# $\mathcal{M}$ONEY IS LOVE

# MONEY IS LOVE
## Reconnecting to the Sacred
## Origins of Money

BARBARA WILDER

Wild Ox Press
Boulder, CO

Second Edition, Revised
Published by Wild Ox Press, 1999.
ISBN 0-9673346-0-8
Second Printing, 2001

First Edition published by Baksun Books/Dristil Press, 1998.

Cover design by JK Cree Design
Cover illustration by Jocelyn Cree
Illustration concept by Lisa Trank
Typeset and designed by Jennifer Asteris
Author's photograph by Patrick Pritchett
Copy editing by Randy Roark

Printed in the UnitedStates of America

Quote from *Breakthrough*, copyright © 1980 by Mathew Fox. Reprinted by permission of Random House, Inc.

Excerpts from *The Mother*, copyright ©1992, 1998 by Sri Aurobindo Ashram Trust. Reprinted with the kind permission of Sri Aurobindo Ashram Trust.

Excerpt from *Your Money or Your Life* by Joseph Kulin. First published in PARABOLA, Spring, 1991. Copyright © by Joseph Kulin. Reprinted by permission of Joseph Kulin.

Quote from *The Four Laws of Actualism*, as taught in Actualism, copyright © 1971 by Russell Paul Schofield and 1986 by The Actualism Trust. Reprinted by permission of Actualism.

Wild Ox Press
2617 Juniper Ave.
Boulder CO.

# ACKNOWLEDGMENTS

I wish to acknowledge Louis and Sandra Bohtlingk along with Elana Freeman, Stanley Messenger and Gudrun Pelham, and David and Aslaug Brittaine, founders of the World Finance Initiative who first brought to my attention the idea that money can be love. Their work is invaluable in the earthing of money as love and care.

I wish to thank Jack and Norma Goverland of Unity of Boulder for supporting this work and sponsoring my inital Money Is Love classes.

I gratefully acknowledge Jennifer Heath for her inspired editing, as well as her encouragement and help in getting this project started.

Loving thanks to my husband, Patrick Pritchett, for his editing and constant love and support; and to my son, Sean Harrison, who has worked with me all his life, as we tried to untangle the spiritual meaning and power of money.

Additionally, Deb Evans, Rick Manville, Jack Greene, Silver Plume, all my students, particularly Janet Root, Jean Bowles, Rachel Boucher, Roger Pearson, and Roxanne DesJardins, who went the extra mile.

*for Patrick and Sean*

*Thought directs energy and energy follows thought.*
—Russell Paul Schofield

# TABLE OF CONTENTS

# INTRODUCTION

*Money is the visible sign of a universal force, and this force in its manifestation on earth works on the vital and physical planes and is indispensable to the fullness of the outer life. In its origin and its true action it belongs to the Divine.*

—Sri Aurobindo

The first time I heard the phrase, "Money is Love," from Stanley Messenger, a British metaphysics scholar, at his eightieth birthday party, I was struck immediately by the simple truth in it. Stanley only mentioned it in passing, but my ears pricked up, and I couldn't get the idea out of my mind. When I asked him later to elaborate on "Money is Love," he just said that he had some friends in Scotland who were working with it.

From that night on I was able to think about nothing but "Money is Love." What did it really mean? I meditated on it and prayed about it.

I've been a student and teacher of metaphysics and light energy for more than twenty years, and for most of those years was aware that abundance and goodwill were synonymous. But it wasn't until the words *money* and *love* came together in that simple sentence that the idea became more than an intellectual conundrum.

The first clue to understanding what "Money is Love" meant came by looking into history. For two years prior to the night I met Stanley, I'd been doing research for a Celtic novel I was writing. In the course of that research I'd become intrigued with the Celts' relationship to gold. Not only was gold related to sun worship, as has long been understood, but the Celts saw gold as the link between the life on earth and the life after death, as evidenced by the wearing of gold *torcs* (necklaces) into battle, often as their only attire. Also, I had come across a reference to a Celtic gold route, which fascinated me. It seemed that this route was not a path of commerce, but more like a sacred way punctuated by temples in which the gold was used for some spiritual practice.

Over the next few months I began putting the idea of "Money is Love" together in my mind with the Celts' sacred beliefs about gold, and what emerged was a new angle on humanity's true connection to money and money's connection to the Divine.

It wasn't an easy leap to make. Though I was immediately attracted to the idea of "Money is Love," I had to overcome my skepticism. After all, in our society equating money with love seemed ludicrous. Metaphysical teacher or not, money and love didn't belong in the same paragraph, let alone the same sentence.

I, like most people, thought of money in the company of other words: words such as greed, fear, lack, anger, hatred, discrimination, multi-national corporations, graft, huge budgets, declining and escalating stock markets, recession, depression, inflation, deflation, angst, hardship, welfare, drug cartels, organized crime, computer moguls . . . need I go on?

I argued with myself that the greatest problem in marriages is money. The greatest motivation for crime is money. The reason for all war, no matter how it's camouflaged in high-minded ideologies, is money.

Yet with all these negatives, I conceded that almost everybody's dreams are about getting money. Even in our daydreams, finding true love usually comes second to getting that magic truckload of money.

One thing seemed clear: we humans have a love/hate relationship with money that is deeply embedded in our psyches. We want money for what it can buy, but at the same time, we think money is bad, dirty, *filthy lucre.*

There I was, stuck on this wild idea that "Money is Love," and at the same time challenged by some very convincing hard evidence that money is anything but. It was at this point that I asked myself — what if this hadn't always been the case? What if the hints I'd received while studying the Celts suggested some alternative mode? What if money hadn't always been devoid of goodness or separated from the sacred? Could money have its roots in the sacred? And if it did, was there some way for money to be reconnected to those roots? This was a radical notion.

I began to research the history of money. I learned that money has changed and evolved throughout human experience, reflecting and expressing each era's worldview.

My research took me from history to pre-history. And it was in the prehistoric that I began to get a real sense of money's original sacredness and its gradual separation from that divine origin.

Today, this separation seems to be complete. Nothing is left in our consciousness that would connect money to the Divine. But just because we aren't aware of money's sacredness, doesn't mean it's not based in truth. What it does mean is that we need to be reeducated so that money can take its place as a tool for goodness in society once again.

Sacredness and divinity are not in themselves easy concepts for the twentieth-century Western mind. But love is something we do understand. In that case, I realized, love must be the connecting emotion, which could help us restore money to its sacred place in the world.

But what did all this mean to individual human beings? After all, as my friends often like to remind me, I'm an idealist who is always looking for ways to save the world. I get carried away thinking about the betterment of humankind in some distant future. I knew I needed to bring this idea down to earth, or off my cloud, as my best friend used to say.

The path to discovering the practical applications of "Money is Love" led me into the world of quantum physics.

I knew from the first time I heard the words "Money is Love" that it held a practical meaning for individual people. But what could it be? And then it clicked. Money is energy. Not just symbolic energy, but literal energy.

I pulled a $10 bill out of my wallet and held it in my hand. It was just paper, but it didn't feel like ordinary paper. That $10 bill was invested with a powerful energy. Was the paper itself energy, or was it the way I thought about the paper that endowed it with energy? Is money energy directed by our thoughts about it? Quantum physicists have begun to understand that human attention focused on particles of energy can influence and change the nature of that energy. According to Russell Schofield, quantum physics can be defined as "Thought directs energy and energy follows thought."

A wonderful truth began to dawn on me. If money is energy and thought directs energy, we must be able to consciously direct the flow of money/energy in our lives. The practical ramifications of money responding to our thoughts were fantastic.

Money, however, isn't just pure energy. Money is energy that has been directed by human thought and consciousness for thousands of years. That is, throughout history, humanity as a collective intelligence has created what money is and how it moves through society. Up until now this has been an unconscious activity. And all human experience and human emotions have been injected into the energy we call money.

Money may have begun as a form of exchange infused with the sacred energy of a divine creator, but it has gotten pretty damned polluted. Today, money carries with it all the fear, anger, and greed that every individual has felt about it as it passed through their hands. Money is dirty, filled with the disgusting, mean-spirited, terrified energy of the human beings whose thoughts direct it.

Money is energy that should flow freely through our lives and throughout the world. But fear blocks the flow. Fear is like a dam. Hoarding, greed, belief in lack and scarcity are all elements of fear, and together they create a great dam that backs up the flow.

So if we human beings have infused money with all this negative baggage, it only stands to reason that we should also be able to clean and infuse it with positive power.

To clean money, to redirect it from the profane to the profound, will take concerted and conscious effort on the part of many individuals. This will happen with one person at a time joining the effort. It is hard work. But the reward is living an abundant life, free of money worries. Sound impossible? It only requires changing our minds.

One by one, as we decide to change money energy from greed, fear, lack, and suffering, into love, joy, abundance, and goodwill, our own circumstances will change for the better. This will happen because the money, free of its old fear-based baggage, will be able to flow. Then infused with its new attributes of love, joy, abundance, and goodwill, the money will infect the way we feel, think, and behave.

Abundance will begin to flow through our lives. Money will simply be there. We will find ourselves working at jobs that have meaning to us. We will find ourselves living in a state of joy. Instead of living in a constant state of fear that there won't be enough to pay the rent or the mortgage, we will even become free to think about how we can share our abundance.

And it all begins with the simple thought: "Money is Love." This may sound like a monumental undertaking. To believe that it can be accomplished by simply changing our thoughts is a difficult leap to make, and to make it we need help.

It has taken us centuries to get this far away from the truth about money. We hold deeply rooted belief systems in our collective social psyches about what money is and how it works. We also carry emotional pain from our personal family histories. To heal, we need exercises and tools.

This new, yet ancient, approach to money is difficult for all of us, from the richest to the poorest. We are all stuck in the mindset that money is scarce and that there just isn't enough to go around. We all believe that even if there's enough now, there might not be enough later.

The fear that we'll lose it all is what causes greed. A greedy millionaire is not greedy because he was born mean and miserly. He is greedy because he is steeped in the fear that he may not have enough later.

The fear the rich person has of losing money is the same fear the poor person has of starving or becoming homeless from lack of money. These fears are different in degree, but not in kind. These fears stem from the false belief that money is finite, that there is only so much money in the world, and that this finite amount is not enough to go around.

The fear that there is not enough money comes from our separation from the sacred aspect of money. In the divine realm, there is abundance for all. But over the centuries, we have created a world of duality, where the material world and the spiritual world have become separated.

We have misinterpreted the Biblical line, "Render therefore to Caesar the things that are Caesar's, and to God the things that are God's." We have taken this as an injunction to separate the physical world from the spiritual world. Yet I believe that Jesus was not talking about money, but about the consciousness surrounding money. When we change the energy around money from fear to love, we bridge the gap between the material and the spiritual world and make it possible for the unlimited abundance of the Divine to flow freely into our own lives and throughout the world.

As we enter the twenty-first century, we stand at a crossroads of human evolution. The traditional ways of problem solving have proved ineffectual. We must find new modes, different mind-sets, new takes on ancient traditions. A powerful tool for accomplishing this transformation is to change money into love.

When money, no longer steeped in fear, greed, anger, and scarcity, but infused with love, joy, abundance, and goodwill, begins to flow through the world, it is quite possible that money itself can become a healing agent that can transform whatever it touches.

I have spent the past few years working with the concept that "Money is Love." I have taught classes about it, and I have seen the gentle miracles it has brought into my life and the lives of my students.

This book may make you angry. But don't be alarmed. Anger is one of the emotions that naturally comes up when the subject is money. Other emotions that may surface as you read about how you can bring a sense of love, joy, and abundance into your money-life are fear, greed, and a sense of lack. In chapter three I address these unpleasant emotions and recommend tools and exercises to process and move through them. On the other side of the anger and fear is an amazing world that is well worth the work it takes to get there.

I realize this is a radical idea, but I ask that as you read this book, you open your mind, let it be free to wander, to imagine the possibilities.

# ONE
# A VERY BRIEF HISTORY OF MONEY

# A VERY BRIEF HISTORY OF MONEY

*Money originally was a storehouse of power. In its most primal sense, what eventually became "money" must have been regarded as magical, something able to translate differences between commodities or services and to reconcile relationships on different levels. Money was a symbol, a metaphor for the divine, the creator, having the power to create, to do. Utilized ceremonially, it had the ability to attract the attention of spirits or gods. . . .*

—Joseph Kulin

I began my journey toward understanding "Money is Love" by looking at money's history. History is one-dimensional, just words in books to many people, but my father taught me that to understand the present and have a vision for the future, we must study the past.

As I paged through conventional books on the history of money, I was disappointed. I was looking for the genesis of money in human culture, and I was only finding essays on early coinage. I realized that like most historians, money historians consider history as beginning around 5000 years ago, when written history began. I was looking for deeper roots. I had to expand my search into the prehistoric. Luckily, the information about prehistory we now have through the work of archaeologist Marija Gimbutus and anthropologist Rianne Eisler, among others, has begun to erase the line that once separated the two eras.

Let's begin by looking back as far as the late Paleolithic, circa 40,000 BCE. During this time our ancestors were tribal hunter/gatherers. We learn from the cave art, as well as from the thousands of small female statues unearthed in archaeological digs all over the world, that these early people worshiped the Mother God who was the spirit of the earth. The earth was considered mother of all, because from her all things were born. Everything necessary to keep people alive came from the Mother Earth. The most significant of these necessities were food and shelter.

For help in acquiring food and shelter, and maintaining life, these ancient peoples prayed and participated in sacred ceremonies to the Great Spirit Mother, as well as the spirits of the animals they hunted and the plants they gathered. Even today, we can witness these same kinds of sacred rituals and ceremonies among remaining indigenous peoples.

This sacred connection between people and the spirit world around them was not an abstract concept to the ancients. All facets of life and death were connected to the sacred spirit world. No hunter left for the hunt without asking for help from the spirit of the earth and the spirit of the animal being hunted. No food was gathered without prayers to the Mother God. Every morsel of food was a sacred gift from Mother Earth.

Moving from the nomadic life of hunters and gatherers into the settled agrarian cultures that began to develop around

9,000 BCE, our ancestors began to hunt and gather less as they created small stationary communities in which they learned to plant crops and raise animals. Nothing was less sacred, but now the rituals and ceremonies centered on planting, harvesting, and domesticating animals. Every seed that was planted was prayed over and blessed. Every harvest was a gift from the Divine Mother.

With settled communities and the domestication of animals came the understanding that the male was an integral participant in procreation. Over the next few thousand years, the Mother God was joined by a son, then a consort, and eventually by male gods. After the male gods were introduced, we moved quickly into the traditionally historic period, approximately five thousand years ago, which culminated with the Semitic one-male god system that is still predominant in the West today.

From the earliest times, trade existed between tribes. The most traded item was food. Because food was sacred, the act of trading it was also sacred.

In the Neolithic agrarian cultures (circa 6000 BCE), grains became the biggest trade item. The rituals surrounding the planting and harvesting of grain during the Neolithic era were the most holy times of the year, and the grain or corn gods were worshiped beside the Mother Goddess. The trading of the sacred grain was a sacred transaction. To cheat in a sacred transaction was to break faith with the Divine, and to do this was not yet part of human consciousness. That would come later, as society became hierarchical. But in the early Neolithic, the sacred connection to the Mother Earth was still intact.

By the time metals were introduced around 4500 BCE, money in the form of grain and other traded foods and items had existed for thousands of years. And during all of this time, money and the interaction between people as they exchanged money were encompassed in the divine realm of the sacred.

When metals were introduced, jewelry, cauldrons, and goblets began to be made from the most precious metals — copper first, then gold and silver. The finest of these metallic art objects were created as gifts for the goddesses and gods. Excavations of bogs that were once sacred pools in Britain have delivered up thousands of golden treasures from the Celtic period. The sense of the sacred in money and monetary transactions lasted well into the historic period when coins were finally introduced.

## GOLD AND SILVER

During the Paleolithic, the moon was the most revered celestial body. The cycle of the moon was the basis for calendars. The earliest, carved on bone, is carbon-dated around 70,000 BCE. In the Neolithic, the sun took its place beside the moon as an equal. Then in the Iron Age, the development of metals caused a very interesting evolutionary leap.

Because human beings had always known the interconnectedness of all things material and spiritual, the discovery of metals only deepened that understanding. The sun and moon were not representatives of gods, but gods themselves. The lunar goddess and the sun god lived within the moon and the sun, not as separate entities, but as integrated spirits. Gold and silver metals were understood to be extensions of the spirits of the celestial divinities.

Let's look at this more carefully. Understanding that gold and silver were considered aspects of the divine sun and moon by these ancient peoples, and not representatives of the sun and the moon as our modern minds are trained to think, is extremely significant.

To understand this concept, imagine yourself as a member of a Neolithic village. Everything in your life depends on the reaping of a good harvest. The sun must shine on the crops all summer long to ensure a good harvest. The god who is the sun must be worshipped and revered to ensure a good harvest. Recently, gold has been discovered and you, knowing that all things in the heavens and on earth are one in the great cosmic dance, now hold a piece of gold in your hands. To you, this is not an inanimate object that shines and reflects the sun's light. This is a piece of the divine sun itself. And the fact that you are holding a piece of God in your hand means that you have a sacred responsibility. To do anything with this piece of the Divine but dedicate it back to the sun god is unimaginable. The gold and silver are part and parcel of the divine sun and moon.

Because of the sacred origin of gold and silver, these metals were initially used only in tribute to the gods. Depending on the culture, the gold and silver were deposited on an altar in a temple erected to the god, or as in Celtic societies, given directly to the goddess or god by dropping the gold and silver in whatever shape — jewelry, goblets, coins — into sacred bodies of water. Wishing wells are a remnant of that ancient practice.

## COINS REPLACE GRAIN

Practicality spurred the use of coins as money. Grain was a fine commodity for trade while people lived in small farming communities and didn't move around too much. But when civilizations began to emerge, armies began to march. A soldier had to be paid, and he certainly couldn't carry stores of grain along with him on a forced march. Slowly, coins were introduced into everyday economics.

By this time, the early historic period (3000 to 2500 BCE) in Egypt and Mesopotamia, abstract thinking began to emerge and with it came humanity's obsession with symbols. This caused a crack in the holy oneness of the Divine and human beings. The spiritual and material world began to separate. As the gulf between the spiritual and the material world widened, money, still wholly sacred, became the connecting bridge between the two worlds. To signify this link between Heaven and Earth, coins were imprinted with the head of a god or a god symbol on one side and a secular symbol on the other.

Money as the link between Heaven and Earth lasted well into the Roman period. But as the spiritual underpinnings of the Roman Empire dissolved, money, for a time, lost its divine connection. The Celtic tribes of Europe still held gold sacred when Julius Caesar conquered Gaul in the first century BCE. Caesar discovered the Gold Route of the Celts, a spiritual path that ran from the gold fields of Ireland through Britain, across the channel and into Denmark and France. The gold was carried from temple to temple along the route enabling the sun's spirit to permeate the earth, divinely commingling the spirits of Heaven and Earth. But the Romans, who had lost all awareness of the sacred realms, saw the gold only as secular wealth. In the next century, they conquered Britain and stole the gold for its material value and burned the temples. In Rome, by the time of Nero's reign in the second half of the first century CE, money had become as profane as it would be until modern times.

After the fall of Rome, around the fourth century CE, European culture returned to a more rural way of life. During the Dark Ages, coinage was scarce among the upper classes and almost non-existent among the peasant classes. Trade and barter again took center stage in the world of money and economics. People were reconnected to the earth as they scratched a living out of the soil.

The medieval Christian Church, which later would falter and eventually succumb to the greed and avarice they advocated against, taught balance between the secular and the spiritual lives of the people. Money was necessary for the material life on earth, but not in place of the individual's search for God. The pagan ways of the ancestors, commingled with the new Christian religion, and money and trade were reinvested with a sense of the sacred. Usury, the act of charging large sums for lending money to individuals, was a sin. People only asked for a loan if they were in dire circumstances, and to take advantage of a person in such straits was considered to be against God's law.

Near the end of the Middle Ages, world commerce emerged, and with it the development of the merchant class and the guilds. Coinage began a resurgence, and paper money was introduced along with checks. During this period and well into the Renaissance, money maintained its sacred connection. As can be gleaned from close study of the painting, "The Money Lender and His Wife" by the sixteenth-century Flemish painter Quentin Matsys (the Louvre Collection), money becomes the third element in a balanced social trinity that also includes family and religion. Though money lending was emerging as a business to support the burgeoning trade industry, the act of usury remained a sin.

It wasn't until the Industrial Revolution that money lost its link to the spiritual realm altogether and came to reside, as it does today, completely in the material realm. At the turn of the millennium, we once again find ourselves in a world not unlike Rome of 2000 years ago, in which money has lost all connectedness to the Divine.

# TWO
# MONEY AS ENERGY

# MONEY AS ENERGY

*The divine circulations never rest nor linger. Nature is the incarnation of a thought, and turns to a thought again, as ice becomes water and gas. The World is mind precipitated, and the volatile essence is forever escaping again into the state of free thought.*

— Ralph Waldo Emerson

For the past 500 years, money has been both coin and paper. Now as we move into the twenty-first century, it is plastic and heading toward "virtual." The most outstanding feature of money since we've moved from the grain standard — whether to coin, paper, or plastic — is that it has no real value. Even gold and silver contain only the earthly value assigned to it by people. And yet money, in and of itself, is extremely powerful. Holding a $100 bill in your hand will give you an instant understanding of just how powerful money is.

Why is this? Why is money powerful? Because money is energy. The energy of money is directed by the collective consciousness of the community. As humanity has become less and less connected to the Divine, we have put more and more of our attention into money — getting money, spending money, hoarding money. Money is no longer a link, a connection with, or an expression of the Divine, but has replaced God. Instead of dedicating money to the Divine, we have made money itself sacred.

How do we turn this around? How do we begin to return money to its sacred place on the planet and in our lives, and in so doing, open ourselves up to the abundant flow of money?

First, we have to understand that what creates our reality is where and how we focus our thoughts; where we put our attention and with what intention. That is, we have to know a little about the principles of quantum physics.

The simplest explanation of quantum physics entails a scientific observation made about twenty years ago. Having inferred the existence of a sub-atomic particles called quarks, the scientists began to look for them. They discovered that although there was no evidence that a quark existed in a place before they'd looked for it there, now that they had, it did. They could only find it when they *intended* to look for it in that specific place. Why, they asked, was the quark there only when they looked for it there? And why hadn't it been there before they looked for it there?

The answer seems to be that the particle of energy known as a quark responds to human thought. Expanding on this, we can either look to the macrocosm or the microcosm. Examining the macrocosm, or the "big picture," we see why quantum physics is making spiritual human beings out of some scientists. The idea that thought can determine the location of particles of energy strongly suggests that some kind of intelligence in the universe directs energy to gather together in different densities to become stars, galaxies, planets, and all the other "things" that seem to exist.

Taking a step down toward the microcosm, we can look at our own world and the people, plants, and animals on it. Some intelligence was necessary to direct all the particles of energy into form — into water, air, wood, earth, etc.

Russell Schofield, a teacher of metaphysics and a man ahead of his time, was aware that physics and metaphysics were one and the same when he said, "Thought directs energy and energy follows thought."

Taking a different step down from the macrocosm to the microcosm of universal intelligence, we come to human intelligence and what effect human intelligence, has on energy. The question then arises: does mass-mind consciousness, the combined thinking of a population, have the ability to create a reality? I believe that the answer is yes.

Take the example of baseball. Baseball is the most beloved of American games. It brings tears to the eyes of millions of Americans and has had the power to do that for over a century. But in the rest of the world, baseball is just another game, which moves no one to tears, or to think of mom and apple pie. On the other hand, in many parts of the world soccer can propel people to equal heights of emotion.

America's love of baseball and other countries' love of soccer are examples of the power of mass-mind consciousness. These two games are just games, nothing more, until the society decides to put its collected *attention* on them with the *intention* of making them extremely important — indeed mythic — in the lives of their respective cultures.

This mass-mind consciousness directs money in the same way. Until human beings put their attention on the pieces of paper in their wallets and collectively direct those pieces of paper to be money, they are not money. They have none of the power of money.

Money is energy directed by our thoughts and can take any form that we collectively agree upon. Therefore, as human culture progressed from money as grain to money as gold and silver, to money as paper, to money as plastic, we as human beings were the directors of the process.

Likewise, it is humanity that has directed money in its evolution from the sacred to the profane.

If we, as a collective, have created the reality that money is scarce, that money is not connected to a higher source, and that money carries with it fear, greed, guilt, loathing, and poverty, why can't we change it?

It is my deep conviction that we can change it. And the way to do it is to change the way we think and feel about money individually.

As one by one individuals change their mind-sets from money as fear, greed, lack, and anger, to love, joy, abundance, and goodwill, the collective mindset also slowly will begin to change. And there will begin to blossom a new understanding throughout the world about what money is and how it flows through individual lives and through the lives of everyone on the planet.

## MONEY MUST FLOW

Because money is energy, it must flow freely. Hoarding stops the flow of energy. Hoarding creates a wall of stopped-up energy. Because money is energy directed by peoples' thoughts, there can be enough money, or there can be not enough money. We have, as a species, collectively decided that there is not enough money for everyone. We have decided that there will be some people who have a lot and some people who have a medium amount and some people who have very little. It is not a fact of the universe that the amount of money in the world is finite. This is rather a condition that we as human beings have agreed to adhere to.

No one stops us from having more money. Whenever the U.S. government wants more money, it prints more money. Whether the printing of more money benefits the country and helps balance the world economy, or causes depression or recession, has nothing to do with the amount of dollars in circulation. It is the psychological state of the majority of the people in the country that determines it.

Currently in Russia, the ruble is almost worthless. Economists say that printing more money will only further deflate the ruble. The truth is that the people of Russia have lost all sense of themselves because their way of life has been devastatingly altered over the past fifteen years. They don't have a stable economy because they don't have a stable way of life. Coming out of a socialist monetary system in which everything was provided by the government, then thrown into a capitalist monetary system where everyone is expected to participate in the movement of money, is an extremely difficult change to make. Until a substantial majority of the people in Russia learn to live under this new system, or until they develop a different system which they feel comfortable living in, the ruble will continue to have little value. The moment the Russian people move into an understanding and acceptance of a new way to live with money, the ruble will gain worth accordingly. This is not to say that the Russian people have brought this on themselves or that there is anything they could have done to stop it. I only use this as an example to show how the collective psychology of a group of people influences the way money flows through a culture.

As individuals and as societies, human beings have the ability to direct the flow of energy in the form of money. We do it all the time. The stock market goes down. The stock market goes up. Economists cloak their explanations in numbers and indices, then mumble a phrase or two about the political atmosphere or the emotional climate of the population. Questioned directly, economists will be the first to say that theirs is not an exact science, and that the stock market is directed by the mood of the country. What they're really saying is that money is energy directed by the attitudes and emotions of the people.

At some point in history, we collectively decided that there wasn't enough money for everyone. And so there isn't. Yet, in studying quantum physics, we learn that energy is not finite. Energy is infinite. Money is energy. Therefore money is not finite. Money, or the energy that is money, is infinite. As individual human beings, we have the potential for understanding this concept and therefore the potential to change our thinking about the way money flows.

Recently, I was at the home of a wealthy man. I asked him what he did for a living. He began to explain that he invested in companies and loaned money for new companies to get started. I interrupted him and said, "Oh, you play with money?" He smiled broadly and agreed. I told him some of the ideas around "Money is Love." He understood immediately, and was very interested to talk further about the subject. During the conversation, when I brought up the idea that money wasn't finite, he exclaimed that I was quite right. "There is enough money for everyone," he told me. "It's just that very few people know it."

Easy for him to talk, he has money. What about the poor slobs who don't? you ask. Yes, it's hard for those who don't have money to believe that there is enough. It takes a leap in faith to believe there *is* enough money for everyone! To make that leap of faith, we have to heal the old mindsets that keep us separated from the unlimited abundance of money in the world. What's the trick? The trick is to reunite money with its spiritual roots. To make money love.

# THREE
# HEALING THE WOUNDS — FREEING THE ENERGY

# HEALING THE WOUNDS — FREEING THE ENERGY

*To receive we must be alert, awake, and prepared to receive.*
—Matthew Fox

Becoming aware of the history of money and the physics of money are the first steps on the road to turning money into love. The next step is divesting ourselves of the deep-seated belief systems that keep us living lives of fear, anger, greed, and scarcity.

We all hold certain beliefs about money, which we learned from our parents. Most of us have parents or grandparents who lived during the Great Depression of the 1930s, a terrible time of national poverty. That mindset of poverty and lack shaped our understanding of what money is from our earliest childhoods.

The puritanical ideology that the Pilgrims brought with them when they landed at Plymouth Rock is another deep-seated belief system that we in the United States all share. This is the doctrine based on hard work, austerity, and excessive adherence to strict moral codes. The idea of "an honest day's wages for an honest day's work" comes from the Puritans. But the facts don't back up that belief. The poor more often than not do an honest day's work and get slave wages, while many corporate executives often do much less than an honest day's work and accumulate fortunes.

People cope with this inequity in various ways. The majority simply accepts the status quo. They do their honest day's work and take home their meager salaries. A small minority resorts to crime, taking what they feel they should have. And another even smaller minority learn the lessons of the rich and break into the ranks of the wealthy.

The belief that every person has the freedom to become rich is another deeply embedded idea in the American spirit, an uncomfortable bed partner for our Puritan ethic. No wonder we have problems understanding money.

All of us carry some amount of this dysfunctional societal monetary mindset in our psyches. To top it off we each carry our own personal money histories.

One of my students wrote, "All through my childhood my dad told me I was worthless....I didn't deserve an allowance. Sometimes when I'd do all my chores, he'd begrudgingly give me a nickel. To this day, fifty years later, I still feel like I'm worthless and that all the work I do deserves only a tiny salary."

Another wrote, "My mother told me that only bad girls worked outside the home. Good girls married good men, who took care of them. I realized while doing my journaling about money, that every morning when I drive to work, I hear my mother's voice in my mind telling me I'm a bad girl."

And another, "My dad was in the military, and he expected all of us boys to follow in his footsteps. I didn't want to go into the military, but my dad said that I didn't have enough talent to do anything else, and that I'd better get used to it and knuckle under or I'd find myself on the streets."

Each one of us has our story. To get to these stories and begin to heal them we need to do some deep soul searching.

## TOOLS AND TECHNIQUES

To heal old stories and belief systems takes work. For this work we need tools and techniques to help us delve into our psyches, discover our blocks to the flow of abundance and free us from them.

### *Journaling*

Journaling is a tool that many teachers suggest for digging up the old mindsets that cripple our current lives. To use journaling to unearth and begin to heal your personal issues around money, choose a time of day when you can be completely alone for twenty minutes.

Get a spiral notebook and a pen that you really enjoy using. Then every day at the appointed time show up to the writing place. This can be anywhere in the house where you feel comfortable. Write with a pen and not on the computer. Put your pen on the paper and write a stream of consciousness for twenty minutes. Don't stop writing. It doesn't matter what you write or how you write it. This writing is for no one to see but you. Don't worry about style or even about punctuation. Just write whatever comes out on the paper. You may wander far from what you consider to be relevant. Allow that. Don't try to control what you write. If you let your hand write, it will begin to uncover things that your brain has never known.

The guidelines for journaling are:

- write by hand
- begin by writing the question, "What does money mean in my life?"
- continue to write without stopping for twenty minutes.

*Note*: It is important to find a safe hiding place for your notebook, because you want to be free to write out all of your feelings. If you are afraid that someone might read your journal, you may subconsciously stop yourself from expressing some important information.

This exercise is an amazing tool. To do it, you need discipline and the courage to show up to write every day. As you begin to uncover painful memories, a new understanding of yourself and the limitations you put on your life will begin to emerge.

One of the first emotions you encounter on this path may be anger. Anger is the greatest block to the flow of abundance. Anger stops everything. But don't let the anger stop you from continuing with the journaling. Plow through it. Don't shove it back down below your awareness. Write it out. And if you need to, as I often do, go someplace where you won't bother anyone and scream it out. You *can* get through the anger to the other side where you will be free of it. Don't stop yourself. But don't take the anger out on others either. This is between you and your spirit.

Other emotions you will encounter are fear, grief, and a sense of worthlessness. These feelings are natural emotions, which everyone has around money. Write them out. Talk to yourself on the paper about how these feelings affect your day-to-day life.

Don't berate yourself for having these feelings. Instead, be gentle with yourself and give yourself gifts. The gifts can be as simple as a new bottle of bubble bath and the time to luxuriate in a hot tub. Or the time to watch a football game on television. Healing one's money problems takes digging up the old fears and pain, and then healing the wounds with self-love.

### Meditation: "The White Light Downpour"

To change money from fear, greed, scarcity, and anger to love, joy, abundance, and goodwill takes a change in consciousness. There is no way that I know of to change consciousness any more powerfully than through meditation. Many people shy away from meditation. The idea of sitting and "doing nothing" with closed eyes is frightening to many people.

On the other hand, closing one's eyes and being very quiet is known to have many beneficial outcomes, such as lowering blood pressure, relieving tension, or lowering the risk of heart disease. In a state of quietude, subtle changes in consciousness are allowed to occur. While meditating we become aware of a universe that is not readily apparent during normal daily activity.

A simple meditation, "The White Light Downpour," has the added advantage of giving the brain something to do while you sit with closed eyes.

To do "The White Light Downpour," sit in a comfortable chair with both feet on the ground and your hands in your lap. Close your eyes and begin to think of gathering all your thoughts into a point in the middle of your forehead. This helps you to disconnect from your daily life and begin to focus. After a minute or so, begin to direct all your collected thoughts, or gathered awareness, back to the middle of your brain, and then up through the top of your head to an area about six inches above your head. This is your Upper Room. It is a place outside the normal everyday world where you can go anytime to relax and renew your spirit. It is a beautiful space that is completely your own.

Take a moment and just look around your Upper Room, relax and enjoy being in it. You may find a big, comfy chair or a window-seat where you might want to sit and read a book. The things you can do in your Upper Room are boundless.

After enjoying being in your Upper Room for a few moments, observe a point of light that is becoming brighter and brighter. A Radiant White Star if forming. You don't have to see it. Many people are not visual and experience their Star with their intuitive "knowing" sense. Just be aware that your Star has been lighted.

This Star is your connection to all the light energy in the universe. Now that you have lighted it, you will be connected to the universal light energy for the rest of your life. Next, remembering that in quantum physics and metaphysics thought directs energy and energy follows thought, direct your Star to open up and begin to pour liquid white light down like rain. The liquid white light pours down through the top of your head, through your brain, your face, into your throat, down through all of your body, down through your arms and legs, and into your hands and feet.

When the light reaches your hands and feet, think of opening up the palms of your hands and the bottoms of your feet and let the light wash on out and down into the earth. As you direct the light to pour through your body, observe and experience the subtle feelings and changes taking place in your body as the light pours through. Wherever you feel any discomfort or pain, direct the light with your thoughts to that area of your body, think of intensifying the light, then allow the pain or discomfort into the light.

After a few minutes of the downpour, direct the bottoms of your feet and the palms of your hands to close. The downpour of liquid white light continues, but now it begins to fill you up. The light fills up your feet, hands, legs, arms, torso, neck, and head, until you are so filled with white light that the light spills out of the top of your head and down the front and back and sides of you.

You are filled now with white light from inside out and from outside in. Float for a few moments in the light.

To end the meditation, move back up into your upper room. Direct the Star to stop the downpour. Take a deep breath. Think of touching with your conscious awareness into your forebrain, into the palms of your hands and the bottoms of your feet, to bring yourself solidly back into time-space. Open your eyes.

This meditation can be done in ten minutes. After awhile you may want to expand it to fifteen or twenty minutes. But ten minutes is a fine amount of time for beginners. And because your brain has something to do, it makes it much easier for your thinking mind to stop fighting the idea of meditation. If you do this meditation directly after your journaling, you will find that the light washes away and heals much of the pain that you are uncovering in your journaling.

### Gratitude

Another powerful tool, and one that must not be overlooked, is to give gratitude. One way to do this is to wake up every morning and, before you get out of bed, stop for a moment and think of one thing you are grateful for. Keep a little notepad, or the journal at the back of this book, next to the bed. When you have thought of what you are grateful for, say it out loud and then write it down. At the end of the week you can read your list of seven things you are grateful for, and begin a new list for the following week. This is a simple tool, but more powerful than you can imagine.

## *Shringing*

One of my favorite tools is what I call "Shringing." Shringing is an ancient mantra to the Hindu Goddess, Lakshmi. As the embodiment of abundance, Lakshmi represents all the Mother Earth has to offer. She is most often depicted standing on a crimson lotus blossom filled with golden coins. From the palm of her right hand more golden coins pour forth. To call Lakshmi and her abundance into your life you simply chant the word "Shring" continuously 108 times. You may chant the word in any pitch or tone. Keeping count is done with Mala beads. Mala beads are a rosary-like necklace with 108 beads, plus an anchor bead. They are often made from seeds or wood, but can be made from any kind of bead, and strung on a heavy cotton thread. You can purchase Mala beads in stores that sell sacred objects or in stores that sell imports from India, Nepal, Tibet, or Thailand. Both Buddhists and Hindus use Mala beads in their prayer practices.

The word-chant Shring is far older than the Goddess Lakshmi. In the Hindu tradition, before there was a pantheon of gods, there was only one God, the Great Mother, and her name was Sri. When you chant "Shring" (sometimes spelled "Sring") you are actually calling the ancient Mother God back into your experience.

Shringing is an extremely powerful tool. Toning, using any repeated sound, opens up a resonance in your body and spirit; it allows you to enter into a deeper harmony with the world and the universe that we are all part of. The sound of the word "Shring" toned over and over works to open your psyche to the resonance of the abundance of the earth.

I have often found that when there is a block to the flow of money in my life, if I Shring two to three times a day, the logjam is cleared within a week or two. Shringing before going to sleep each night works to help the flow move naturally in our lives. It is also very relaxing. It seems to allow the body and soul to harmonize into a peaceful place from which sleep naturally flows. I highly recommend using this tool on those nights when money worries are keeping you awake. My husband and I try to Shring together every night before sleep. We find that it not only alleviates money worries, it helps relax all the tension built up over the day. And as we relax and tone together, we naturally fall into a loving and harmonious state with each other.

### *Prayer*

Prayer remains one of the most powerful tools in the world. What is prayer? Taking time out to be very still and talk directly with the Divine. You may do this in any way that feels most comfortable to you. I have written a *Money is Love Prayer*, which appears on page 85. You may use this prayer, write your own prayer, or simply ad-lib your prayer. But make sure when you are praying to remember that you are a part of this great and abundant planet and universe, and that there is a plan for your life. The Divine isn't sitting up on some distant cloud waiting to make bargains with you. The Divine is deep within your own soul, lovingly nudging you toward recognition of your own divinity. Once we recognize our own divinity we are able to see, more and more clearly, the part that we play in out own destiny. Prayer helps us get to this point. Pray daily to enter into the abundant flow of the universe and watch the floodgate open.

### Examining Money

For this exercise you will need a $1 bill. Our twentieth-century American dollar bill still includes both the secular and the spiritual symbols that were found on the earliest imprinted coins. The potential for money linking the material and the spiritual realms still exists, not only in theory, but also in the very practical reality of the dollar bill itself. Pick the dollar up and look at it closely. On the front side you'll see a picture of George Washington, some designs, the number one, some long serial numbers and a couple of signatures as well as the words *FEDERAL RESERVE NOTE*. Not very interesting.

Now, turn the dollar bill over and examine the back side. In the center just above the word "ONE" is the phrase "In God We Trust." To the right is a circle with the American eagle, the secular symbol of our nation. On the left is another circle. In this circle is a pyramid with an eye replacing the point of the pyramid. This is called the Eye of Horus, which in ancient Egyptian mythology was the "all-seeing eye of God."

Above the pyramid are the Latin words, *Annuit Coeptis*. Translated, this means "He has favored our undertakings." Below the pyramid are the Latin words, *Novus Ordo Seclorum*, or "New Order of the Ages."

With the knowledge that money is energy and our dollar bills actually contain the symbolism of the sacred and the mundane, we can begin to change the energy that money has in our lives by changing the energy of every dollar that moves through our hands.

### *Laundering Money — The Spiritual Way*

As people spend money, they consciously or subconsciously harbor the fear that the money they are spending could be the last money they will ever have. The energy around the money becomes charged with this fear. Considering how many hands money passes through and how much fear it picks up along the way, it's no wonder money is scarce in so many lives. Who wants to handle all that fearful negative energy? But what if money felt good? One way to make money feel good is to clean it.

This next exercise is a cleaning tool. It requires a quiet, private place and a dollar bill. Pick up your dollar bill. Hold it between your hands. Close your eyes. Collect your thoughts, go into your upper room and turn on your White Star. Direct the white light energy down through your body, down your arms and into your hands. Open the palms of your hands and direct the white light into the dollar bill. As you do this, imagine the white light energy cleansing and purifying the dollar bill. As this continues, begin to repeat, either silently or out loud, the affirmation, "Money is Love." Do this for a few minutes. The longer the better, but don't overdo it. When you feel that the exercise is over, stop.

## Wallowing in Money

This exercise requires ten or twenty $1 bills. It should be done alone in your bedroom or in the middle of the living room floor. First, hold all the money in your hands and do the purifying or money laundering exercise. Cleanse the money with the white light energy and repeat the affirmation, "Money is Love." Think of yourself as an ancient alchemist changing the nature of money from fear to love.

Next, spill the clean, lighted dollars out on the bed or the floor. Look at them. Pick them all up and throw them into the air. Lay them all out in a straight line. Make a design with them. Crumple them up. Smell them. Spread them out around you. And finally, roll around on them. Feel the lusciousness of high-energy love-money.

## Spending Money AS Love

This exercise has two parts and requires the ten or twenty $1 bills that you have cleansed and alchemically changed from fear to love.

**Part One:** Take half of the purified dollars to a favorite shop and buy a little gift for yourself. The article you buy should not be something you need but something that is a luxury. As you begin the act of handing the money to the clerk, think the thought "Money is Love." Then release the money to the clerk. Be strongly aware that this clerk now holds a handful of money that is infused with love and not fear. Realize that you have given a stranger several units of love. Try to become aware that this person is being impacted in a subconscious way by the act of receiving money charged with love and not fear. Remain consciously involved with the transaction. Watch the clerk put the money into the cash register. Send one more thought that money is love, as the money is put into the cash drawer.

**Part Two:** Take the other half of the dollars, which you have purified and charged with love, and give it to a street-person. As you hand the money to the person, remain conscious of the fact that you are giving units of love. Stay in that feeling throughout the transaction.

*Warning:* Do not let your thoughts and feelings include anything but the idea that you are giving another human being money infused with love. Don't let yourself move into any judgment of the person, or any arrogance about being better than the person to whom you are giving the love money.

## Tithing

Tithing and charity are two different things, which is important to understand as you begin to work with the concept that "Money is Love." Tithing, not uncommon among religious groups, is the act of giving a sizeable percentage (traditionally 10%) of your monthly income to persons, institutions, or organizations you admire for their positive works toward the betterment of the planet and/or the human race.

There are two important elements in tithing. The first element is to give more than you think you can afford. This forces you to put your faith in a spiritual source and thereby expand your abundance level. The second element is to give upward; that is, to give to people or organizations that are more highly evolved in their understanding of the spiritual nature of money and its connection to divine source.

Charity, on the other hand, is giving what you can afford to those who are in need. Though acts of charity are often positive, charity has the potential to have negative qualities. One negative quality inherent in charity is the ease in which the giver can move into a false belief that he is in some way better than the recipient. This sets up arrogance in the giver, while simultaneously setting up a sense of worthlessness in the recipient.

Also, when you give to someone or some organization because they are experiencing scarcity, you are supporting lack. When you give because you believe a person or organization needs it or because they can't make it without you, you are giving to and empowering lack in the others and yourself.

Tithing more than we think we can afford forces us through our fears by demonstrating abundance. In so doing, it allows us to open to the divine flow of money, love, abundance, and goodwill. Tithing helps us break the old habit of scarcity in our lives. To break any habit one must first act "as if" the old habit no longer exists.

### Tithing Money AS Love

"Money is Love" consciousness adds to the power of tithing and eradicates the negative aspects of charity. By changing your money into the energy of love, every dollar you tithe already exists on a higher spiritual vibration, and therefore intensifies the power of your tithe. Charity given from the place in consciousness that money is love, joy, abundance, and goodwill, allows both the giver and the recipient to connect to a powerful spiritual current — a current of goodwill and abundance.

When money is love, every monetary transaction is tithing. When you distribute all of your money on a flow of love, joy, abundance, and goodwill, every dollar you send out into the world travels in the sphere of divine grace. Each person who receives your money receives it on a divine and spiritual level, as well as on the material level. This means essentially that every dollar you spend on anything goes directly to the Godness within whomever receives the money. This makes virtually every monetary transaction you do in the spirit of "Money is Love" a tithe.

For example, when you pay your electricity bill with money transformed into the energy of love, joy, abundance, and goodwill, you are sending that love, joy, abundance, and goodwill to the electrical company. You are saying "thank you" for giving you electricity this month. You are acknowledging the gift of electricity with the payment of the bill in love-money energy.

An angry student once asked me how he could be expected to send money as love to the Internal Revenue Service after the way they had screwed him. I replied that if all your money has been infused with love, there is no way you won't send money as love to the IRS. And the IRS will become the recipient of a powerful infusion of love and gratitude.

From here, I told him, you must make the leap to accepting as truth the fact that "everything that goes around comes around." If you send out money infused with love and abundance to everyone, only love and abundance can come back. This is the law of the universe. What you put out comes back to you, directly or indirectly, but it always comes back to you.

### *Writing "Money is Love" on Your Checks and Credit Card Slips*

One of the simplest and most effective tools is to write "Money is Love" on all your checks and credit card slips. On checks, I write it on the memo line in the bottom left corner, but you can write it anywhere on the check. On my credit card slips I write it directly under my signature.

The benefits of writing "Money is Love" on your checks and credit card slips are two-fold. The first, I'll discuss here. The second, I'll discuss in the chapter five.

When most people write a check, they go into fear mode. You may or may not notice that this happens to you, but as you become more actively aware of your relationship to your money, you will notice fear is involved somehow when writing a check. The most usual way of dealing with this fear is to slip into unconsciousness. You go into overdrive. You write without being conscious. In other words, you push the fear into the back of your mind, the pit of your stomach, or the back of your neck. By the end of a day of shopping and writing checks, you wonder why you have a headache, a sore neck, or a stomachache.

The day every month when I paid the bills, I aggravated my old neck injury the most. I would hunch up over the checkbook, tense every muscle in my body and write the checks. Even after I'd been on a spiritual path for many years and thought I knew that money was part of spiritual abundance, I still got the sore neck.

Writing the words "Money is Love" on the bottom of the checks makes you stop for a moment and breathe. It takes about four seconds to write these three little words, but the benefit is well worth the little extra time.

Think about the last time you were at the supermarket. You're standing in front of the grocery clerk. The people in back of you are in a hurry. You're writing the check as fast as you can. You're sure you've spent too much, but you've just got to pay it and get out of there. You have to have food. You shouldn't have bought that expensive jar of olives. Maybe you should have bought the healthier cereal. Your husband is going to be mad when he sees the grocery bill this month. Your wife is never going to understand why you spent so much on that great-looking roast. Your kids are going to be angry at you for not buying the snacks they asked for. All of this is going on in your mind as you write a check for much too much money, and on top of everything else, you didn't watch the cash register and maybe you were charged too much for something that was on sale.

Stop. Breathe. Take four seconds to write the words "Money is Love" on the memo line. Write it all out. Don't cheat and write MIL. When you take the time — four little seconds — to write these three words, an amazing thing happens. You release the fear. All of the anxious little voices in your head stop. They have to. You're concentrating on writing the affirmation, and you can't be bothered with them. It's only four seconds, but after you've done this you realize you feel better. You didn't know you felt bad, but suddenly you realize that you feel better. You are consciously directing yourself out of your subconscious fear cycle.

Everytime I describe this tool at least one anxiety-ridden student asks me, "But what will the clerk say if he sees 'Money is Love' on the bottom of the check?"

The first answer is: "Why do you care?" The second answer is, in my experience, most clerks don't say anything. More often than not, clerks don't even read what you've written on the memo line. It's not part of their job. When clerks do read the line, some smile and nod, others choose to ignore it. And once in awhile, a clerk will ask me what it means. When that happens, a dialogue has been opened and I am able to say something simple like, "It's an affirmation that helps turn money from fear and lack to love and goodwill." Every clerk I have ever told this too has responded in some positive way. Usually with just a knowing smile.

One young man at my local liquor store looked at the words "Money is Love" on the bottom of my check, then looked back at me and said, "Oh, I get it. When your checks come back in your bank statement, you get all that love."

"Right," I answered. "And as I hand you this check, I'm handing you love."

"Cool!" He said and smiled.

It is also important to write "Money is Love" on your bank deposit slips to send money as love into your own personal bank account.

Using these few simple exercises will help you begin to change the way you perceive money. And very subtly, money will begin to become more abundant in your life. To this will be added a greater sense of freedom and a greater sense of joy in your life.

Don't expect overnight miracles, but when one occurs, be accepting of it. Miracles come in all shapes and sizes. Most miracles are small and difficult to detect with our twentieth-century brains that are accustomed to huge, noisy images splashed across mega-movie screens and hundred-foot billboards. But changes in consciousness are most often gentle and displayed in nuances appreciated by our much more delicate sensibilities.

Be gentle and open to this part of yourself, and you will begin to see that money can be love, joy, abundance, and good-will in your life.

# FOUR
# THE THREE G'S — GREED, GUILT, OR GUT

# The Three G's — Greed, Guilt, or Gut

As you begin to work with the tools and exercises, it will seem as though you've opened up Pandora's box, and the first reaction will be to find the lid and close it as quickly as possible. But if you put the lid back on the box, you won't be able to heal, and if you don't heal you won't be able to live an abundant life. One of the most difficult things for we human beings to do is to focus our attention on our money. The reason it is so hard to focus on money is because of the fear, lack, greed, and anger that infect it. But turning our backs isn't the answer. To heal the money-wound in our lives we have to be courageous.

Stepping onto the path of healing our relationship with money is a heroic stance. And like all heroes, we have to leave the safety of our normal lives and journey into the special world where the dragon — our fear, anger, grief, and pain — resides. Once there we must gather all of our strength and courage to go one on one with the monster. The fight is never easy, but with perseverance and a willingness to believe that we're not alone, that we're part of a Divine Oneness, we will win. Having overcome our fear, we can return to our normal lives as a conquering hero carrying the elixir, the magic potion, back to our home-hearths like the heroes of myth. And remember, no hero ever conquered a dragon that she refused to acknowledge existed.

The slaying of the money-dragon is a process. It doesn't happen in one fell swoop. It happens day by day. We begin to notice subtle differences in our attitude toward money. Slowly our fears begin to have less power over our thoughts. Gradually we begin to put our trust for support and abundance, not in the outer-directed world, but in the world of the sacred and its Divine abundance. Enjoy and savor each little change, for these changes are the steps toward your freedom and your enlightenment. Celebrate each new revelation. No one ever gained true abundance by winning the lottery. It is in the small, almost unnoticeable, moments that our abundance begins to flow and our healing happens.

As we begin to heal our issues around money, an interesting question arises. How much money *is* an abundant amount of money? Most people's response to that question goes something like this (the amounts may vary), "I need a million dollars, so I can invest it, and make sure it grows into several million dollars, so that I will have enough money to get the kids through college and have a secure retirement."

Our brains and our outer-directed thinking, which has driven our accumulation of money in the past, are trained to think in finite terms. To our limited minds, an abundant amount of money means a solid amount of cash. But money is energy. And energy is neither solid nor finite. To try to harness a chunk of this constantly flowing stream of energy is impossible. We believe in a fantasy, devised by the human mind, that there is a finite amount of money in the world, and we must struggle, often to the point of death, to get our chunk of it. This, of course, is the very thinking that has created the lack of abundance in our society and in our lives. We must come up with a different solution.

Beginning with the awareness that money is energy that flows constantly though the world, and having at least a modicum of faith that there is enough abundance for everyone at all times, we can begin to understand that the amount of money we need to live an abundant life depends on many factors. And because our lives are constantly changing, the amount of money we need changes too. Added to this is the fact that we are each unique, individual human beings. This means our needs will be different from our neighbor's needs, a fact that seriously destroys the logic of "keeping up with the Joneses."

There are different timetables in our lives, and we have different monetary needs for all of them. When we're raising children, our needs are very different than when we've just gotten out of school and are living as young singles. After the children are grown, our money needs change yet again. But these are just the broad strokes of our lives. Every day is different. We have certain monthly bills, the rent or the mortgage, the car payment, food, but above and beyond these basic survival expenses, there are months when we need more money, when there is a big event, a vacation, a new pair of glasses, a wedding gift. And then there are the needs of our souls — the drawing class you want to take, the ski trip you've been dreaming of, the dress that is way too expensive for your budget but will soothe your soul and help you get over the guy who just dumped you, or the job you just lost.

And then there are the times when we don't need as much money. When life isn't so taxing. When we've finished paying off the car, and really don't need a new one yet. When the kids are finally on their own and actually paying their own way. When we don't really want to go to a fancy restaurant, but would just like to sit home and read a book.

The hardest thing to learn is that we can't control the future. Many people I know are struggling with retirement plans. Planning is a good thing, to an extent. But living under the illusion that you can predict what will happen in your life, what your needs will be, how the politics of the country will evolve, what the inflation rate will be over the next twenty years is completely impossible. There is no way to know these things, and yet people sit up night after night, trying to second-guess the unknowable, to plan for a secure and predictable future. No wonder the stress level drives so many of us to early heart attacks. We are trying to control a limitless universe with a very limited set of ideas and a finite amount of money.

To become more in tune with the natural flow of the money in our lives, we have to begin to listen to the Divine voice within us. There is a part of us that some call the Soul, and others call the Higher Self, or Spirit. I call this my Teacher/Knower, the eternal part of me who knows why I'm here, what lessons I need to learn in my life, and just about anything else. It is through meditation and journaling that we begin to learn how to listen to this inner guidance.

Many days we may wake up worrying about the lack of money for a specific thing that we think we need. The worry seems to take on larger and larger proportions as the day goes on. We must find a way to get the money. What if we don't get the money? What will happen to us? What will people think of us if we don't get the money? If we don't pay the mortgage, the rent, the credit card bill? If we can't buy the prom dress, take the vacation? The worrying leads us to fear. The fear leads to obsessive worry. The "Idea of Lack" looms larger and larger in our mind's eye. Soon we begin to feel small, worthless, not good enough to be with others, who we are sure have more than us, and are therefore more worthy. And as we spiral down further and further into the sense of worthlessness, we begin to become angry. We begin to feel rage at those who have enough. For those who have more than we do. And then we begin to plot our revenge on the "others." And it is at this point that we reach the extreme separation from the Divine Oneness. And divided from our truth we wallow hopelessly in unbridled anger and eventually despair.

Pulling oneself up out of this pit is difficult. Sometimes it can seem almost impossible, and for some it is. But what if we stopped the cycle at the beginning and nipped the fear in the bud at the first sign of worry? If we could do that, we wouldn't have to spend so much time and energy on spiraling downward and then dragging ourselves up out of the abyss.

The tools in the previous chapter are designed to help you keep yourself out of the downward spiral that leads from worry to despair. And what I call "**The Three G's**" is a kind of measuring device to help put the brakes on. The Three G's stand for Greed, Guilt, or Gut.

To apply this measuring device you must start by remembering that everything in the universe is in a constant state of flux, that nothing will be the same tomorrow, and that all you must do to get to tomorrow is to live through today. Then, using journaling, meditation, or prayer or better, all three begin to examine exactly what it is that you truly need for **today** — **NOT TOMORROW** — just today. Do you have what you need for today? If you don't have what you need for today, what is it that you need?

Once you think you know what you need, it is time for the Three G's. Working with the Three G's helps you to experiment with your feelings. To start, ask yourself if what you believe you need is based on Greed? And by Greed I mean your fear that there is never enough, and so you must have more than you actually need. Ask yourself if you can really get by with less than what the Greed has led you to believe.

If your need for today passes the Greed test, go to the next step, Guilt. Maybe you are experiencing a sense of Guilt based on whatever issues from your past you haven't healed yet. Your actual need may be much greater than what you have even dared to think about. Maybe this sense of guilt is keeping you from being able to allow the necessary money in. Using your tools, examine this gently and compassionately.

The final G is for Gut. You've seen your own greedy wants, and you've examined the guilt-driven lack. Now you are free to move toward your truth, the feeling in your gut that tells you what you truly need today. What do you need to live a full, abundant day? Allow your mind to wander and let your feelings come to the surface. Perhaps this is a day of ebb. A day when the flow is moving out to gather more force for the next high tide. Perhaps your Gut is telling you to relax, ease up. This isn't a day to go out and TRY to get money. Or maybe your Gut, your inner voice, is telling you to get up out of bed, stop feeling sorry for yourself, and do something for someone else. Or maybe your Gut is telling you to get up, eat breakfast, go to work, and let the Divine take care of things for today.

Tune in! Is it Greed? Do you need that new car because your neighbor just bought one, and you have to have as much, or more, than she does? Or do you need that new car because your old car won't support your soul's needs anymore?

Is it Guilt? Are you driving an old beater because you don't feel like you deserve a nice car? Or are you driving an old beater because you don't really care about cars that much and are saving up for a trip to Alaska, which will fulfill a lifelong dream of living like a pioneer?

Is it Gut? Are you living each day of your life based on the deep needs of your Soul? Are you paying attention to the subtle ways in which you are learning to stretch toward your own true sacredness?

How much money do you need for your own sacred growth and development? Use "The Three G's" to help you decide this, one day at a time.

# FIVE
# MONEY IS THE BLOOD OF THE PLANET

# Money is the Blood of the Planet

Everyone who applies the principals and begins the process of changing the energy of money from fear, greed, lack, and anger, to love, joy, abundance, and goodwill will find themselves living a happier more abundant life. And this is a good thing. But this personal benefit is only half of the concept of "Money is Love." The other half is the promotion of Money *as* Love throughout the planet to help heal relationships between nations, to stop war, end hunger and disease, and heal the environment.

A big order? Yes. But possible. The most destructive force in our world today is money. Those who have it want to keep it, and those who don't have it want to get it. This promotes crime, war, hunger, pollution, and disease. No political solution has been able to quell the spread of these scourges. Nor has any religion.

Because people are steeped in the mind-set that there is only so much money, we continue to hold onto the belief that there are only so many who can have enough to live abundantly. And therefore they must take it from others. This is a concept devised by what Riane Eisler, in her seminal book, *The Chalice and the Blade*, calls the "dominator society."

A dominator society is one in which there are dominating and dominated members. We are currently living in a dominator society and have been for the past 5000 years. We have come to believe that this is the only kind of society that can exist. But Eisler puts forth that, before the dominator societies, there existed partnership societies; that is, societies in which men and women shared equally in all things. Communities in partnership societies were governed in a partnership fashion, and therefore had no need for dominator chieftains or kings. In these societies there were no slave or servant classes.

During this pre-dominator era, money was handled by the sacred ones. In some Native American tribes the shamans own nothing, thus keeping the handling of money pure.

Now, as we move into the twenty-first century, we are at a crossroads in the evolution of humankind. We have the opportunity to forge a new kind of society. To do that, we need to change our concepts around money.

As individuals, we have learned through reading this book and working with the tools and techniques that we can change our concepts around money. But the question arises, what about the people in developing countries and less affluent communities? "Sure," you say, "I can sit here in the United States as a member of the middle class and change my life. But what about the people overcome by famine in Africa? The children in the ghettos of Philadelphia or Los Angeles? The Amazon tribes being disgorged from their ancient homes, while the land is deforested for corporate agriculture?"

Money *as* Love has the power to affect every person in every corner of the world. The principle is very simple, and yet at the same time, difficult to comprehend.

Money circulates the planet constantly. It changes form from dollars into rubles and lire, etc. as it crosses borders, but it continues to circulate. This is the nature of money. Money — like the rivers and streams — flows throughout the planet and everything it touches it affects in some way, just as the rivers and the oceans affect every part of the planet that they touch.

In the human body, blood flows throughout the body, never stopping, unless there is disease. Blood carries the nutrients throughout the body to keep the body healthy. When the blood is diseased, the body becomes diseased.

Money flows through the world as blood flows through the body. Money carries with it the ability to provide for all the world's needs, but when it is diseased, the entire world becomes diseased. To heal a person with a blood disease, the blood must be healed or a transfusion given so that healthy blood can flow throughout the body, bringing with it the properties needed to heal the rest of the body.

When the energy that is money is infused with fear, greed, anger, and scarcity, it flows throughout the world carrying these destructive properties and infecting all that it touches. Since money touches everyone, no matter how remote their village, the people of the world, the communities they live in, and the land they live on are polluted with the disease of fear, lack, greed, and anger.

If one by one, we as individuals begin to change the money that moves through our hands and our bank accounts into love, joy, abundance, and goodwill, the money itself becomes healed. Like a blood transfusion, we will begin to infuse the money supply of the earth with love. Then the love-infused money will begin to infect the entire money supply of the world. When Money *as* Love begins to circulate, it affects the population and the healing process begins. This world community, which is in the process of destroying itself with money, can actually use the very tool of destruction to heal itself.

This is where the other benefit of writing "Money is Love" on your checks and credit card slips comes in. When you distribute money, in the form of checks and credit cards with the words "Money is Love" written on them, you are sending the healing power of love into the bloodstream of the planet and actively healing the money flow.

Money is the blood of the planet. Heal the money, and we can heal the world. Because there is no lack or scarcity in money that is infused with love, the leaders of Wall Street and the multinational corporations will not be threatened. There is enough for all. As individual people — shop owners, bankers and even, eventually, corporate leaders — begin to embrace this idea, more and more Money *as* Love will begin to circulate.

As each dollar, yen, ruble, or Euro-dollar is infused with love, joy, abundance, and goodwill, the people it touches will be lifted into a more loving state of existence.

The idea of a change like this sounds incredible. Impossible. Ridiculous. The skeptics among us will say that even if the theory is correct, there is no way to get all of the people to transform all of the money into love. And that's true. But it doesn't take all of the people. Change happens when enough people have joined the new mind-set. In science this is called "reaching critical mass." Critical mass takes only a fraction of the whole to shift the balance just enough to get the ball rolling in another direction. The rolling ball picks up speed the farther it goes until, suddenly, change occurs. Miracles can be achieved when individuals change their thoughts about money from fear, greed, anger, and lack to love, joy, abundance, and goodwill.

The great Indian master, Sri Aurobindo, says "The money-force has to be restored to the Divine Power and used for a true and beautiful and harmonious equipment and ordering of a new divinized, vital and physical existence, in whatever way the Divine Mother herself decides in her creative vision. But first it must be conquered back for her. . . ."

By changing money to love in your own consciousness, you are becoming a facilitator of this divine mission.

# Money is Love Prayer

Universal Divine Source,

I take this time to open myself and my life to your abundance.
The abundance that flows freely through this honorable universe.
The abundance that is for the many, not just the few.
The abundance that is my birthright as a divine being on the path
toward enlightenment.

Help me to learn that money is not separate from you, but is part
of you, as I am part of you, and you are part of me.
Help me to learn that money is an integral part of my spiritual
lesson-learning.
Help me to learn that money is not mine to control.

Teach me to begin to change my attitude toward money.
Teach me to see money as energy that can be transformed into love,
So that each dollar I send out into the world flows from me on a
current of love and light.
So that each dollar I send out into the world can touch another person
with love.

As I go forth each day, help me to open my heart and my mind
to the possibility that I truly can change my concept
of money, from the negative ideas I have about it into
the concept that Money is Love.

For this and all the abundance you bring into my life each and every day,
I am deeply grateful.

So be it.

# GRATITUDE JOURNAL

## WEEK ONE

Day 1: I am grateful for_____

Day 2: I am grateful for_____

Day 3: I am grateful for_____

Day 4: I am grateful for_____

Day 5: I am grateful for_____

Day 6: I am grateful for_____

Day 7: I am grateful for_____

## WEEK TWO

Day 1: I am grateful for_____

Day 2: I am grateful for_____

Day 3: I am grateful for_____

Day 4: I am grateful for_____

Day 5: I am grateful for_____

Day 6: I am grateful for_____

Day 7: I am grateful for_____

## WEEK THREE

Day 1: I am grateful for_____

Day 2: I am grateful for_____

Day 3: I am grateful for_____

Day 4: I am grateful for_____

Day 5: I am grateful for_____

Day 6: I am grateful for_____

Day 7: I am grateful for_____

## WEEK FOUR

Day 1: I am grateful for_____

Day 2: I am grateful for_____

Day 3: I am grateful for_____

Day 4: I am grateful for_____

Day 5: I am grateful for_____

Day 6: I am grateful for_____

Day 7: I am grateful for_____

## WEEK FIVE

Day 1: I am grateful for_____

Day 2: I am grateful for_____

Day 3: I am grateful for_____

Day 4: I am grateful for_____

Day 5: I am grateful for_____

Day 6: I am grateful for_____

Day 7: I am grateful for_____

## WEEK SIX

Day 1: I am grateful for_____

Day 2: I am grateful for_____

Day 3: I am grateful for_____

Day 4: I am grateful for_____

Day 5: I am grateful for_____

Day 6: I am grateful for_____

Day 7: I am grateful for_____

## WEEK SEVEN

Day 1: I am grateful for_____

Day 2: I am grateful for_____

Day 3: I am grateful for_____

Day 4: I am grateful for_____

Day 5: I am grateful for_____

Day 6: I am grateful for_____

Day 7: I am grateful for_____

## WEEK EIGHT

Day 1: I am grateful for_____

Day 2: I am grateful for_____

Day 3: I am grateful for_____

Day 4: I am grateful for_____

Day 5: I am grateful for_____

Day 6: I am grateful for_____

Day 7: I am grateful for_____

# NOTES

_____

_____

_____

_____

_____

_____

_____

_____

_____

_____

_____

_____

_____

_____

_____

_____

_____

_____

# NOTES

# NOTES

# NOTES

# BIBLIOGRAPHY

Baring, Anne and Jules Cashford. *The Myth of the Goddess*. London: Viking Arkana, 1991

Cameron, Julia. *The Artist's Way.* New York: G.P. Putnam's Sons, 1992

————. *The Vein of Gold.* New York: G.P. Putnam's Sons, 1996

Eisler, Riane. *The Chalice and the Blade*. San Francisco: Harper & Row, 1987

Fox, Matthew. *Breakthrough*. New York: Image Books, Doubleday, 1980

Hyde, Lewis. *The Gift: Imagination and the Erotic Life of Property.* New York: Vintage Books/Random House, 1983

Kulin, Joseph. "Your Money or Your Life" *Parabola Magazine: Money, vol. XVI, Number 1*. February 1991

MacCulloch, J.A. *The Religion of the Ancient Celts*. London: Studio Editions, 1992

Markale, Jean. *The Celts: Uncovering the Mythic and Historic Origins of Western Culture*. Rochester, Vermont: Inner Traditions International, 1978

Needleman, Jacob. *Money and the Meaning of Life*. New York: Currency/Doubleday, 1991

Ross, Anne and Don Robins. *The Life and Death of a Druid Prince: The Story of Lindow Man, an Archaeological Sensation.* New York: Summit Books, 1989

Schofield, Russell Paul, and Carol Ann Schofield. *The Basic Principles of Actualism.* San Diego, CA: Actualism Trust, 1971

Smedstad, Phillip. *How Tithing Prospers You.* Taos, New Mexico: Theophilus Publications, 1989

Sri Aurobindo. *The Mother.* India: Sri Aurobindo Ashram Trust, 1974

Weatherford, Jack. *The History of Money: From Sandstone to Cyberspace.* New York: Crown Publishing, 1997

Zukav, Gary. *The Dancing Wu Li Masters: An Overview of the New Physics.* New York: Bantam Books, 1979

# MONEY IS LOVE
# WORKSHOPS AND LECTURES

Barbara Wilder is available to teach workshops
and deliver lectures based on this book.

**To arrange a workshop or lecture
you can reach Ms. Wilder**

**by phone: 303.444.5963
by email: BarbaraWilder@moneyislove.com**

**Visit our website: www.moneyislove.com**

---

## THE WHITE LIGHT DOWNPOUR

The meditation in Chapter Three,
"The White Light Downpour," is based
on the teachings of Actualism.

To learn more about Actualism visit
the Star Path website at
www.actualism.org